INSECTS

Sarah Wilkes

WORLD ALMANAC® LIBRARY

Please visit our web site at: www.worldalmanaclibrary.com
For a free color catalog describing World Almanac® Library's list of high-quality books
and multimedia programs, call 1-800-848-2928 (USA) or 1-800-387-3178 (Canada).
World Almanac® Library's fax: (414) 332-3567.

Library of Congress Cataloging-in-Publication Data

Wilkes, Sarah, 1964-
　　Insects / by Sarah Wilkes.
　　　　p. cm. — (World Almanac Library of the animal kingdom)
　　Includes bibliographical references and index.
　　ISBN 0-8368-6211-2 (lib. bdg.)
　　1. Insects—Juvenile literature.   I. Title.
QL467.2.W54   2006
595.7—dc22　　　　　　　　　　　　　　　2005052629

This North American edition first published in 2006 by
World Almanac® Library
A Member of the WRC Media Family of Companies
330 West Olive Street, Suite 100
Milwaukee, WI 53212 USA

This U.S. edition copyright © 2006 by World Almanac® Library. Original edition
copyright © 2006 by Hodder Wayland. First published in 2006 by Hodder Wayland, an
imprint of Hodder Children's Books, a division of Hodder Headline Limited, 338 Euston
Road, London NW1 3BH, U.K.

Subject Consultant: Judith Marshall, Natural History Museum
Editor: Polly Goodman
Designer: Tim Mayer
Illustrator: Jackie Harland
Picture research: Morgan Interactive Ltd and Victoria Coombs
World Almanac® Library art direction: Tammy West
World Almanac® Library editor: Carol Ryback
World Almanac® Library cover design: Jenni Gaylord

Photo credits: (t) top; b (bottom); l (left); right (r).
Cover photograph: the face of a tree wasp.
Title page (clockwise from top left): stag beetle, dragonfly, ladybug, wasp.
Chapter collage (top to bottom): macro photographs of the scales on four
butterfly wings and a compound eye.
CORBIS: Robert Pickett cover. Ecoscene: / Robin Williams 6; / Julian Partridge 7; / Wayne
Lawler 14, 40; / Kjell Sandved 18; / Chinch Gryniewicz 25; / Erik Schaffer 42; / Tom Ennis
43. Ecoscene / Papilio: / Peter Bond 8; / Robert Pickett 10, 16, 17, 24(b), 27, 29(t), 31, 34,
37, 38; / William Dunn 11; / Alastair Shay 15; / Lando Pescatori 26, 28; / Michael
Maconachie 32, 41; / Mike Buxton 33; / Robert Gill 35; / Peter Bond 36(t); / Ken Wilson
36(b). naturepl.com: / Ingo Arndt 4; /Richard Bowsher 9; / Dietmar Nill 12; / Solvin Zankl
13; / Duncan McEwan 20; / John B. Free 21; / John Cancalosi 22; / Peter Oxford 23; / John
Downer 24(t); / Peter Blackwell 29(b); / Mark Payne-Gill 30.

Printed in China

1 2 3 4 5 6 7 8 9 10 09 08 07 06

CONTENTS

It is not possible to include information about every insect species in this book.
A taxonomic chart for insects appears on page 44.

WHAT ARE INSECTS?

Insects are the most numerous and diverse of all animal groups. They are found everywhere in the world, from the tropics to the poles. Scientists have identified at least two million insect species, but they believe there may be more than ten million different insect species in all.

Shared features

Insects belong to the phylum Arthropoda—animals with jointed legs. Arthropods have a tough outer layer, called an exoskeleton, covering their body. Their legs are divided into many sections so they can bend easily. All insects have three body parts: a head, a thorax, and an abdomen. Three pairs of legs and, usually, two pairs of wings are attached to the thorax. The head bears a pair of compound eyes, a pair of antennae, and mouthparts that are adapted to each insect's diet.

Metamorphosis

Insects lay eggs that hatch into larvae. The larvae undergo a number of molts before they become adults. The change from larva to adult is called metamorphosis. Some insects have four stages of change—egg, larva, pupa, and adult—called complete metamorphosis. The larva looks very different from the adult. During the pupal stage, the body of the larva changes into that of the adult. Other insects have only three stages of change—egg, nymph, and adult—called incomplete metamorphosis. After each molt, the nymph gradually becomes more like the adult.

The three body parts of an insect—the head, thorax, and abdomen—are easy to see on this young grasshopper.

CLASSIFICATION

Biologists have identified several million unique organisms. They examine the similarities and differences between organisms and group together those with shared characteristics. The classification system moves through general to specific categories until each organism receives an exact binomial classification: a "last" name—the genus—and a "first" name—the species. The animal kingdom is divided into phyla (singular: phylum). Each phylum is divided into classes (also super- and subclasses), which are divided into orders (also super- and suborders) and then into families, genera (singular: genus), and finally, species. A genus and species names a single organism—such as a monarch butterfly—that differs from all other organisms. In most cases, only members of the same species can reproduce with each other to produce fertile offspring.

A monarch butterfly is classified in this chart.

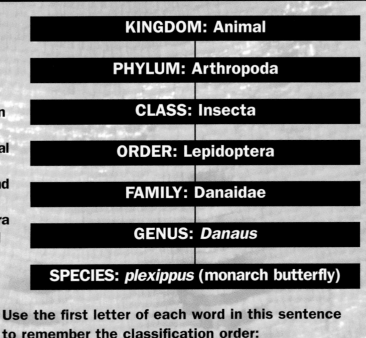

KINGDOM: Animal

PHYLUM: Arthropoda

CLASS: Insecta

ORDER: Lepidoptera

FAMILY: Danaidae

GENUS: *Danaus*

SPECIES: *plexippus* (monarch butterfly)

Use the first letter of each word in this sentence to remember the classification order:
Kings Play Chess On Fridays, Generally Speaking.

COMPLETE METAMORPHOSIS

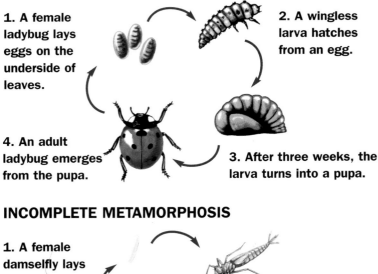

1. A female ladybug lays eggs on the underside of leaves.

2. A wingless larva hatches from an egg.

3. After three weeks, the larva turns into a pupa.

4. An adult ladybug emerges from the pupa.

INCOMPLETE METAMORPHOSIS

1. A female damselfly lays tiny eggs in pondweed.

2. An egg hatches into an aquatic larva (nymph), which goes through a series of molts.

3. The larva spends two years in the water before climbing out. Its skin splits and a winged adult emerges.

The class Insecta is divided into two subclasses: wingless insects (Apterygota) and winged insects (Pterygota). Apterygota contains primitive, wingless insects that do not go through metamorphosis. The subclass Pterygota consists of winged insects that go through metamorphosis. Pterygota has twenty-seven orders that are divided into two groups: Exopterygota, which undergo incomplete metamorphosis, and Endopterygota, which undergo complete metamorphosis.

This book looks at some of the orders of insects, their characteristics, and the way each group of insects is adapted to its environment. A taxonomic tree of the classification system appears on page 44.

WINGLESS INSECTS (APTERYGOTA)

The subclass Apterygota contains about six hundred species of primitive insects that are very different from other insects. The subclass is divided into two orders: bristletails (Archeognatha) and silverfish (Thysanura). The name *Archeognatha* means "ancient jaw." The name *Thysanura* means "fringe tail."

Apterygota features

Unlike all other insects, bristletails and silverfish do not undergo metamorphosis. The young insects, known as nymphs, look like small adults. They develop by shedding their exoskeleton and growing larger.

Bristletails and silverfish do not have wings. They are small insects about 0.4–0.5 inches (1–1.5 centimeters) long. Their bodies are long, flat, and tapered. Three projections, called cerci (singular: cercus), that extend from the end of the abdomen make their bodies look longer. In bristletails, the middle cercus is the longest, but in silverfish the cerci are the same length. Bristletails have particularly long antennae. In addition to three pairs of legs, bristletails have several pairs of short knobs on the abdomen that may be the remains of additional legs lost through evolution.

The silverfish (*Lepisma saccharina*) gets its name from its covering of shiny scales. Young silverfish resemble adults except they are smaller and white. They turn silver when about six weeks old.

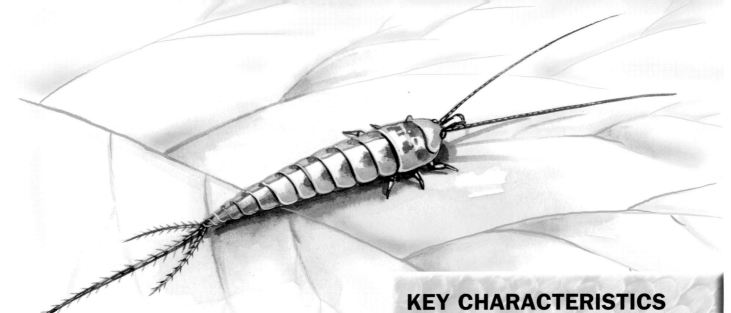

The bristletail is named after the bristlelike hairs that extend from its abdomen.

A strandline marks the high-tide line along a shore. It attracts bristletails and other scavengers that feed on dead sea life and rotting seaweed.

Habitats

Bristletails are often found in grassy or woody habitats. They live in leaf litter—the layer of fallen leaves and twigs that carpet the woodland floor—or under bark and stones. They are nocturnal insects, which means they are active at night. Bristletails are herbivores. They feed on plant matter such as algae, moss, and lichen, but they will also scavenge on dead and decaying animal material in leaf litter. Some types of bristletail live on beaches in the pile of debris that marks the extent of the high tide. This is known as the strandline, and bristletails scavenge for food there.

Silverfish are frequently found in houses, especially in kitchens, bathrooms, and basements, where it may be damp. They are often found hiding under carpets, too. Like bristletails, silverfish are nocturnal, emerging at night to feed.

DRAGONFLIES AND DAMSELFLIES (ODONATA)

Dragonflies and damselflies are brightly colored insects found near water. They are among the fastest insect fliers. They are also among the oldest. Fossil remains suggest that they existed three hundred million years ago. Dragonflies and damselflies are grouped in the order Odonata, which means "toothed jaws." There are more than fifty-five hundred species divided into two suborders, dragonflies (Anisoptera) and damselflies (Zygoptera).

The large eyes of this southern hawker dragonfly (*Aeshna cyanea*) occupy much of the head. Its wings are held out to the side of the body.

Odonata features

Dragonflies are larger and have a thicker body than damselflies. Both have two pairs of large, transparent wings that cannot be folded away. The hind pair of wings on a dragonfly is slightly wider than the front pair. Each pair of wings moves independent of the other pair when flying, allowing the insects to hover and steer in order to catch prey. Damselflies have two pairs of wings of similar size. They hold their wings over their body when resting.

Damselflies, such as this banded demoiselle (*Calopteryx splendens*), have a long, slender body with wings that close above the body.

Compound eyes

Nearly all insects have a pair of compound eyes. A compound eye consists of thousands of tiny hexagonal units, called ommatidia, with their own lenses. Each ommatidium functions as a separate, miniature "eye" that sees only a small part of the entire view. The images received from all of the ommatidia become one view inside the insect's brain. Insects do not see details, but detect colors, patterns, shapes, and movement. The dragonflies' large compound eyes consist of approximately thirty thousands units, giving them excellent sight. They can judge distances and are sensitive to the slightest movements, which helps them fly at high speeds through an array of obstacles in pursuit of prey.

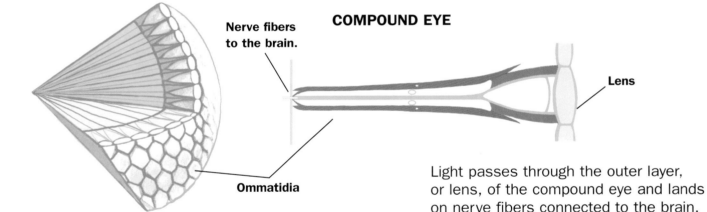

COMPOUND EYE

Nerve fibers to the brain.

Ommatidia

Lens

Light passes through the outer layer, or lens, of the compound eye and lands on nerve fibers connected to the brain.

WHAT'S THE DIFFERENCE?

DRAGONFLY

- **Enormous eyes cover top and sides of head.**
- **Wings held straight out beside the body when at rest.**
- **Strong flier.**
- **The nymph is heavy and moves slowly across the mud at the bottom of ponds, lakes, and slow-moving streams.**

DAMSELFLY

- **Eyes do not cover top and side of head.**
- **Wings held folded back above the body when at rest.**
- **Weak flier.**
- **The nymph is slender and lives in pondweed near the surface of a body of water.**

Dragonfly nymphs have a strange lower lip, called a mask, that can extend to catch passing prey. The mask has hooks along its edge to help grab the prey.

Life cycle

Dragonflies and damselflies undergo incomplete metamorphosis. They lay their eggs in freshwater ponds, lakes, and streams. The eggs hatch into aquatic nymphs that undergo a series of molts. After each molt, the aquatic nymph, called a naiad, becomes darker in color and looks more like the adult. When the mature naiad finally climbs out of the water, it sheds its old exoskeleton, revealing a new one with wings.

Nymph life

The nymphs of dragonflies and damselflies have gills and breathe by taking oxygen from the water. This larval stage lasts between one and five years. During that time, the naiads are carnivorous, feeding on a wide range of aquatic animals, from tiny insects to tadpoles. They catch their prey using an extension of the lower lip, called a mask. This mask resembles a crab claw with two hooks on the end. The naiad lies in wait and then shoots out its mask to grab passing prey. It pulls the prey to its jaws, pumps digestive juices into its victim, and then sucks up the body fluids.

Adult life

Adult dragonflies and damselflies live only about one month. Just like the nymphs, they are aggressive predators—except, unlike the nymphs, they hunt in the air instead of the water. Once they have spotted suitable prey, they give chase. Sensory hairs on the back of a dragonfly's head aid its flight by sending information to the brain about the position of its head relative to its thorax. As it closes in on prey, the dragonfly opens its dangling legs to form a basket to catch the prey.

Hawker dragonflies, such as the emperor dragonfly, patrol stretches of water looking for small flying insects. These large dragonflies will sometimes tackle butterflies. The darter dragonflies employ a different hunting technique. They perch on a plant stem and watch for prey, then dart out to catch it.

Extra order: Mayflies (Ephemeroptera)

Mayflies look very similar to damselflies, with a slender body and wings that close over the body. The adult and nymph have three distinct, slender extensions from the tip of the abdomen. The nymphs spend between four months and three years in the water. They are herbivorous, scraping algae from stones and pondweed. Adult mayflies live only for a few days, in which time they must mate and lay eggs. Many are eaten by fish and birds within hours of emerging from the nymph stage.

The final stage in the metamorphosis of a dragonfly occurs when the naiad pulls itself out of the water. It shed its exoskeleton to reveal an adult body with two pairs of wings.

GRASSHOPPERS AND CRICKETS (ORTHOPTERA)

Grasshoppers and crickets belong to the order Orthoptera. They are found in most land habitats around the world except for the very coldest ones. *Orthoptera* means "straight wings," which refers to the parallel sides of the forewings of these insects.

Orthopterans are best known for their loud chirping sounds often heard on sunny summer days and warm evenings. The Orthoptera order consists of more than twenty thousand species, including grasshoppers, locusts, crickets, katydids, and mole crickets.

Orthoptera features

The distinctive feature of this order is the extra-long pair of hind legs designed for jumping. These long legs are about three times longer than the other two pairs and are equipped with powerful muscles. All six legs have claws that help the insect grip plants.

Orthopterans have two pairs of wings. The front pair is narrow and leathery, and when the insect is at rest, they cover the hind wings. The hind wings are large, very thin, and almost transparent. Although these insects can fly, they are more likely to jump, using their wings to help them

The forewings of Orthopterans, such as this blue-winged grasshopper (*Oedipoda caerulescens*), are held out of the way of the hind wings, which have a much larger surface area for flying.

travel farther. Most orthopterans have a pronotum—the upper surface of their thorax extends forward over the head.

Singing

These insects produce their songs by a process called stridulation. This involves rubbing one part of the body (the file) over another part (the scraper). The file has pegs or ridges that hit the scraper to create the sounds. It works somewhat like a person running a comb over the edge of a playing card. The scraper is always on the wing, but the file may be on the leg (as in grasshoppers) or on the opposite wing (as in crickets). Each species has its own distinct "song." The sounds come in bursts or chirps of varying lengths. The volume and pitch vary, too. Some of these songs might sound like lawnmowers, sewing machines, or even chainsaws! Most of the songs are produced by males to attract females. Female grasshoppers also sing, but their song is quieter than that of the males.

Pests

Grasshoppers and locusts have powerful mouthparts with sharp jaws that are designed to eat tough plant foods. Many of these insects are considered pests because they occur in large numbers and feed on crops, causing a lot of damage. Swarms of locusts regularly appear in parts of Asia, Africa, and North America, destroying all crops in their path. Mole crickets are major pests of the lawns and golf courses in the southern United States. They live underground in long burrows. Mole crickets use their enlarged forelegs like a pair of pruning shears to snip through grass roots.

KEY CHARACTERISTICS
ORTHOPTERA

- **Extra-large pair of hind legs for jumping.**
- **Two pairs of wings, of which the front pair is narrow and thickened.**
- **Pronotum is large and saddlelike.**
- **Incomplete metamorphosis.**

A female mole cricket (*Gryllotalpa* sp.) lays eggs in a small underground chamber. Unlike other species of mole crickets, the Gryllotalpa female visits the chamber to take care of her eggs and hatchlings.

MANTIDS AND COCKROACHES (DICTYOPTERA)

Cockroaches are unpopular insects because most people associate them with dirt and disease. The majority of cockroaches are wild and do not live or feed near people. Cockroaches are closely related to mantids—insects that catch prey using their long, spiny front legs.

Mantids and cockroaches make up the order Dictyoptera, which means "net wing." This refers to the pattern of veins on these insects' forewings. Dictyoptera is divided into two suborders: Mantodea, the mantids; and Blattodea, the cockroaches. Both groups undergo incomplete metamorphosis.

A female burrowing cockroach (*Blattodea* sp.) digs a burrow for her egg case. It contains between twelve and forty eggs that develop underground for up to twelve months.

Mantids

Most of the two thousand or so species of mantids live in tropical areas. They are often called praying mantises because they hold their forelegs as if in prayer. The triangular head contains powerful jaws. Mantids are the only insects able to turn their head to look behind them.

Predatory mantids

Mantids are found in a wide variety of habitats, including grasslands and woodlands. They are usually camouflaged to blend in with their surroundings, so they are difficult to spot. For example, the nymphs of the flower mantis are shaped and colored to look like the flowers in which they live.

- Two pairs of wings. The leathery forewings are held over the hind wings.
- Long, slender antennae.
- Large pronotum: elongated in mantids; shield-shaped in cockroaches.
- Incomplete metamorphosis.

Mantids are predators, feeding mostly on other insects. Some of the larger species tackle prey as large as frogs and lizards. Their camouflage helps them surprise and catch prey. Mantids remain still while waiting for prey to pass. When they spot a suitable prey animal, they turn their head to look straight at the animal. Then, in a sudden movement that lasts a mere fraction of a second, the mantis reaches out and grabs the prey with its forelegs.

Cockroaches

Cockroaches are an ancient group of insects that first appeared on Earth more than three hundred million years ago. At that time in Earth's history, scientists believe cockroaches outnumbered all other flying insects. There are far fewer cockroaches in the world today and most live in the tropics. Of the four thousand known species of cockroaches, only about thirty are considered pests. Cockroaches look somewhat like beetles, with a similar pair of leathery forewings covering

The praying mantis is a killing machine with quick reflexes and spiny, grasping legs that grip prey.

While beetles have forewings that meet exactly in the middle, the forewings of cockroaches overlap, and the female cockroach is often wingless. The cockroach body is broad and flattened, and its legs are long and spiny. It has a prominent, shield-shaped pronotum that extends forward to cover most of the head. A cockroach's sensitive antennae are particularly long. It has large, compound eyes and two conspicuous cerci at the end of its abdomen. A tough egg case protects the eggs. After a number of weeks, the eggs hatch into nymphs, the small, wingless versions of the adults.

BIGGEST AND SMALLEST

- The largest known cockroach in the world, the *Megaloblatta longipennis* from Central and South America, has a wingspan of up to 7 inches (18 cm).
- The species *Macropanesthia rhinocerus* from Australia has the largest body, weighing up to 1.8 ounces (50 g).
- The smallest known cockroach is *Attaphila fungicola* from North America, which is only 0.2 inches (5 mm) long.

Scavenging cockroaches

Although most cockroaches are nocturnal, a few are diurnal (active during the day). The majority live on forest floors, but they are also found in caves and homes. They rely on their antennae to find their

The Oriental cockroach (*Blatta orientalis*) prefers warm places, such as kitchens, laundry rooms, and closets. They emerge at night to scavenge in the dark for food.

way around. Nearly all cockroach species are scavengers that feed on almost anything. Some specialized species feed solely on wood. Wood is indigestible to most animals, but these cockroaches have single-celled organisms living in their gut to help them digest the wood.

Extra order: Stick and leaf insects (Phasmida)

Stick and leaf insects are often called walking sticks because they resemble sticks, twigs, or leaves. The nearly twenty-five hundred species are divided among eight families. Their green or brown coloring matches the plants in which they hide, and their elongated bodies can reach lengths of 11 inches (28 cm). Stick and leaf insects spend much of their time hanging motionless in plants, shrubs, or trees. When they do move, they simply sway slightly, as if caught by the movement of the wind. They have powerful jaws well suited to eating plant leaves. If attacked, the phasmida insects can shed their legs—which grow back again when they molt.

This stick insect has a green body and an outline that blends perfectly with the surrounding leaves. It is almost impossible to spot unless it moves.

TERMITES (ISOPTERA)

Termites are easily confused with ants, but they are more closely related to cockroaches. Termites are described as social insects because they live together in huge colonies. They are found mostly in the tropical and subtropical areas of the world.

A queen termite is surrounded by workers bringing her food. The queen is so large that she cannot move.

Termites belong to the order Isoptera, which consists of approximately twenty-three hundred species grouped in seven families. *Isoptera* means "equal wings," which refers to the similar shape and size of these insects' two pairs of wings.

Living in colonies

Termites live in large groups, called colonies. Each colony can have as many as several million individuals. There is a single queen, a number of kings, and thousands of immature worker and soldier termites. The kings and queen are long-lived, in some cases with a life span of up to fifty years, while the workers and soldiers live for only four years. The mature queen has a huge, bloated abdomen up to 4 inches (10 cm) long. Her role is to lay thousands of eggs each day. The eggs develop into new workers (which are blind) and soldiers.

Termite workers and soldiers can be either male or female. The workers collect food for the queen, kings, and soldiers and tend to the nest. These blind workers find their way back to the nest by following a scent trail laid down on the outward journey. The massive heads of the soldiers are packed with muscles that work their curved, black jaws. Their role is to protect the colony. The proportion of workers to soldiers depends on the needs of the colony. If the colony is constantly being attacked, more soldiers are produced. If the nest needs attention, more workers are produced.

Some termites feed on wood and plants, but most feed on fungi that they grow in underground gardens. The termites bring plant material, such as sections of leaves, into the nest, and the fungi grow on this—just like a compost heap. The termites feed on the fungi.

Massive nests

Termites are the master builders of the insect world. The workers build a nest that extends above and below ground by sticking mud together with saliva. The mound of some nests rises 23 feet (7 m) or more above ground level. The egg chambers and larvae are located deep underground, close to the food stores and fungal gardens. A chimney, which is part of the mound's ventilation system, runs up through the middle of it.

Termite air-conditioning: As hot air from the mound's underground chambers rises through the central chimney, cool air is drawn in to replace it.

KEY CHARACTERISTICS
ISOPTERA

- Chewing mouthparts and short antennae.
- A worker termite has a pale, soft body and a small head.
- A soldier termite has a large head and powerful jaws.
- A queen termite is the largest animal in the mound and has a huge, enlarged abdomen.
- Incomplete metamorphosis.

Termite Mound

mound

chimney

fungal gardens

royal cell with queen and king

brood chambers with eggs and larvae

Earwigs (Dermaptera)

The earwig was named after the superstition that it crawls into people's ears as they sleep and bores into their brains. This is false, of course, but many earwigs are considered pests because they feed on vegetables, fruits, and flowers.

The order Dermaptera consists of about nineteen hundred species of earwigs found around the world. Earwigs range in size from 0.2–0.8 inches (5–20 millimeters) in length. They are colored brown to black. The word *Dermaptera* means "skin-winged," which refers to the insects' soft hind wings. The earwigs' most distinctive feature is their forceps, or pincers, which are modified cerci at the end of their abdomen. Earwigs use their forceps to catch prey and to mate. Although these forceps make people think earwigs are dangerous, they are harmless to humans. Females have straight forceps. Males' forceps are curved and more elaborate.

Earwigs have an elongated body. Many species are wingless. The winged species have a pair of small forewings that meet in the middle and cover and protect the hind wings. The hind wings are much larger, fan-shaped, and thin, and must fold many times to fit under the smaller forewings. While some winged earwigs are strong fliers, not all of them fly regularly.

The earwig (*Forficula auricularia*) raises its forceps over its body when threatened.

Life cycle

Earwigs undergo incomplete metamorphosis, with three stages of growth. The earwig is unusual in the insect world because the female takes good care of her eggs and nymphs. The female lays up to eighty eggs in the soil, which she cleans and guards. The eggs hatch into tiny nymphs that grow and molt, becoming more like the adult. The female cares for her nymphs until they mature.

Nocturnal activity

Earwigs are nocturnal. During the day, they shelter in moist, shady places under woodpiles, stones, boards, and in compost piles or flower beds. They also like to hide in potted plants and flower heads. They come out at night to feed on plants and scavenge for dead and decaying matter. They can become a nuisance in gardens if they damage vegetables and flowers.

At times, large numbers of earwigs gather together and suddenly migrate to a new area. The earwigs might move into cropland or invade homes during prolonged spells of hot, dry weather.

Some newly hatched earwigs. The nymphs are small, with pale, soft exoskeletons.

KEY CHARACTERISTICS
DERMAPTERA

- **Modified cerci that resemble a pair of forceps or pincers.**
- **Winged earwigs have a small pair of forewings and a large pair of hind wings.**
- **Incomplete metamorphosis.**
- **Female earwigs care for their eggs and nymphs.**

Bugs (Hemiptera and Homoptera)

Many people think the word *bug* refers to all insects. The term should be used only when referring to a particular type of insect.

True bugs are sucking insects found all around the world, on land and in water. They range in size from a few millimeters to more than 4 inches (10 cm) long. Bugs undergo incomplete metamorphosis. The nymphs look almost the same as the adults, except they are much smaller and wingless.

Bugs are classified in two closely related orders: Hemiptera and Homoptera. Hemiptera contains about thirty-five thousand species, including bedbugs, shield bugs, and water striders. Homoptera is a slightly larger order, with about forty-five thousand species, including leafhoppers, cicadas, and aphids.

Bugs have piercing and sucking mouthparts. Some suck plant juices, while others are carnivorous and can bite humans and other mammals. The two orders of bugs, Hemiptera and Homoptera, include the most destructive species of insects.

Often called thorn bugs because of their distinctive, thorn-shaped pronotum, treehoppers belong to the order Homoptera.

Hemiptera

Hemiptera means "half wing" and refers to the fact that part of the forewings is toughened and hard, while the remainder of both forewings and all of the hind wings are membranous (flexible). Both pairs of wings are folded over the flattened body at rest. This order also features characteristic mouthparts consisting of four needlelike stylets that rest in a groove called the rostrum. The sensitive tip of the rostrum detects suitable feeding sites. It guides the stylets to the right place and then withdraws as the stylets are inserted into an animal or plant. Food is sucked up through the stylets.

KEY CHARACTERISTICS
HEMIPTERA AND HOMOPTERA

- **Sucking mouthparts.**
- **The forewing of Hemipterans is part hardened and part membranous.**
- **The forewing of Homopterans is either all hard or all membranous.**
- **Incomplete metamorphosis.**

Homoptera

Homoptera means "same wing" and refers to the undivided forewings that are either stiff or completely membranous. When the bug is at rest, it holds its wings like a roof over its body. The mouthparts of Homoptera lie below and behind the eyes, making it look as if they arise from the back of the head or from between the front legs.

The assassin bug (*Reduviidae* sp.) belongs to the order Hemiptera. This large, predatory bug catches, kills, and then sucks the body fluids from its victim with its mouthparts.

Habitats

Bugs are found in almost all habitats, including ponds, forests, and even in our beds! Water striders and water measurers have adapted to living and feeding on the surface of water. Their long legs distribute their weight so that the water's surface tension supports them, and they do not fall into the water. Water striders "row" across the water's surface using their middle legs. Their hind legs trail and act as rudders, leaving their front legs free to catch prey. These insects have hairs that are sensitive to vibrations and help them find struggling insects that have fallen into the water. Water measurers have an elongated head, which is more suited to their method of catching prey. They spear animals that live in water, rather than catching animals on the water's surface.

The adult bedbug (*Cimex lectularius*) is about 0.2 inches (5 mm) long before eating. After a meal, its body becomes swollen and elongated.

BEDBUGS

Bedbugs share some people's beds. During the day, they hide in crevices in floors, beds, or mattresses. They emerge at night to feed on humans by piercing the skin and using their long mouthparts to suck the blood. Female bedbugs lay about two hundred eggs around the bed. Eggs hatch within a few days, and the young bedbugs start feeding immediately.

A water strider (*Gerris lacustris*) has caught a bee trapped on the water's surface. The struggles of the bee created ripples in the water, which alerted the water strider to its presence.

Communication

Cicadas are among the world's noisiest insects. Male cicadas have special sound-producing organs, called tymbals, on the sides of their abdomen. Each tymbal is attached to an internal muscle, which it pulls in and releases. As the tymbal pops back into position, it produces a sound. During warm summer weather, males produce their loud song, which can be heard up to 1 mile (1.5 kilometers) away. The song attracts females and warns off other males.

Pests

Many bugs are plant pests. Aphids, or greenflies, are one of the most destructive bugs. This tiny, soft-bodied bug feeds on sap from plant stems. Aphids insert their piercing stylets into the plant stem and suck out the sugar-rich sap. This reduces the plant's growth and may even kill it. Aphids reproduce rapidly, so a few aphids can soon turn into an infestation.

The mealy bug is another pest that feeds on plant sap. Heavy infestations of mealy bugs may seriously weaken a plant. The female mealy bugs disfigure the leaves or fruit with a wax produced during reproduction. The female mealy bug is hardly recognizable as an insect because it is often wingless and legless.

Aphids are just a few millimeters long. The wingless, adult female aphids produce fifty to one hundred eggs. An aphid egg becomes a reproducing adult within about one week. It produces up to five eggs per day for up to thirty days.

BEETLES (COLEOPTERA)

This seven-spotted ladybug (*Coccinella septempunctata*) raises its spotted wing cases to reveal delicate flying wings underneath.

Beetles have the most species of any type of insect. There are about 370,000 known species, but more are being discovered all the time, especially in habitats such as tropical and temperate rain forests.

Beetles are found all around the world and in a wide variety of habitats. Up to twenty different species of beetles might live in a typical backyard. One hundred or more species might live in a few square yards (square meters) of rain forest. Some of the more familiar beetles include ladybugs, stag beetles, dung beetles, and weevils.

KEY CHARACTERISTICS
COLEOPTERA

- **Tough outer wing cases cover the hind wings.**
- **Powerful biting jaws.**
- **Complete metamorphosis.**

Coleoptera features

Beetles belong to the order Coleoptera, which means "sheath wings," and refers to the toughened forewings, or wing cases. The wing cases lie over and protect the delicate hind wings that beetles use for flight. Wing cases are often brightly colored. For example, the cardinal beetle has red wing cases, and the jewel beetle has sparkly wing cases. Another feature of beetles is the powerful jaws for biting and chewing. Weevils have slightly different heads compared with other beetles. Their head extends forward to form a rostrum, which carries the mouthparts.

Moving fast

Although most beetles can fly, they spend little time in the air. Instead, they tend to stay on the ground or on plants, hunting for food. Some species of ground beetles do not have hind wings and are restricted to life on the ground. Their legs are longer than other beetles so they can chase insect prey. Australian tiger beetles, a type of ground beetle, are among the fastest runners of the insect world, and can run about 5.6 miles (9 kilometers) per hour. In contrast, many smaller species of beetles that live in crevices and under bark have short, stubby legs that are more suited to squeezing into tight places.

Life cycle

Beetles undergo complete metamorphosis with four stages: egg, larva (maggot), pupa, and adult. Most larvae are pale, soft bodied, and live in soil. Some, such as the larvae of ground beetles, are active predators that feed on small insects. Other beetles, such as dung beetles, supply their larvae with dung to feed on. Legless weevil larvae are surrounded by their food of plant roots.

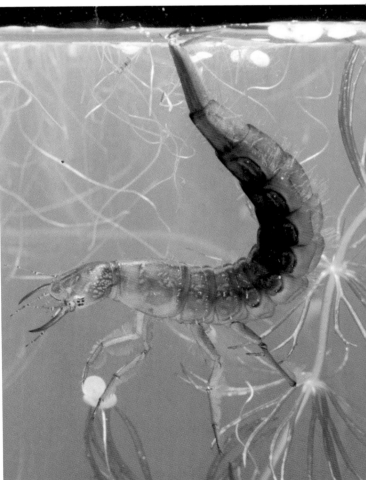

The aquatic larva of the great diving beetle (*Dytiscus marginalis*) pushes its tail above the water's surface to take in oxygen.

Survival

Beetles are a very successful order of insects. Their success comes from their tough exoskeleton and protective wing cases. They can squeeze under stones and leaf litter without injury, survive in dry environments, and use their large hind wings to fly.

Desert beetles

Many beetles live in harsh environments, such as deserts, where there is a shortage of water. Their exoskeleton not only protects their body but also reduces water loss. Most desert beetles have long legs that keep their body from contacting the hot sand. Some species have also evolved unique ways of obtaining water. For example, in southwest Africa, the darkling beetle of the Namib Desert climbs to the top of sand dunes in the morning to collect droplets of water from the mists that roll in from the South Atlantic Ocean.

BEETLE FACTS

- One in every three insects is a beetle.
- Although stag beetles look scary, the heavy antlers of the males are used only for fighting other male stag beetles.
- The devil's coach horse is a type of rove beetle. It gets its name from the way it raises its abdomen up like a scorpion when threatened.

The male stag beetle (*Lucanus cervus*) has mouthparts with enormous jaws. Despite their fearsome appearance, the jaws are useless for biting. They are used only to fight other male beetles.

Aquatic beetles

Aquatic beetles, which live underwater, must obtain oxygen somehow. Adult beetles, such as the great diving beetle, trap bubbles of air under their wings so they can breathe while submerged. Hairs on their hind legs help propel their body through the water. Aquatic larvae have gills to remove oxygen from the water.

Finding food

Most beetles are herbivorous. A number of species, such as scarab, stag, rove, and carrion beetles, are scavengers that feed on the dead and decaying bodies of animals and rotting vegetation. Many of these scavenging beetles lay their eggs on rotting vegetation to ensure that their larvae have a plentiful food supply. Carrion beetles lay their eggs on the bodies of dead animals, while dung beetles lay their eggs inside balls of dung.

Longhorn beetles infest trees. Females chew through the bark to lay eggs in the wood. The larvae tunnel through and damage the wood as they feed and mature. Some predatory beetles, such as ground beetles, feed on a wide variety of small animals, including other insects. Their jaws are designed to grip and kill prey animals and then chew up the bodies.

This great diving beetle (*Dytiscus marginalis*) has caught a tadpole. These predatory beetles also feed on small fish and aquatic insects.

The scarab beetle (*Scarabaeidae* sp.) is a type of dung beetle. It shapes freshly laid dung into a huge ball and then rolls it into an underground nest. The female lays a single egg inside each ball. When the eggs hatch, the larvae feed on the dung.

FLIES (DIPTERA)

Flies are probably one of the least-liked group of insects. Most flies annoy people and animals, and some species spread diseases. Flies belong to the order Diptera, which contains more than 120,000 different species. Flies are found almost everywhere in the world.

Flies range in size from midges that are just a few millimeters long to crane flies with a wingspan of 2–2.4 inches (5–6 cm). This large order includes fruit flies, houseflies, hoverflies (flower flies), and mosquitoes. It is divided into two suborders, according to the length of the antennae. The flies of the suborder Nematocera, such as mosquitoes and crane flies, have long, delicate antennae, while members of the suborder Brachycera, such as blowflies and houseflies, have short, stout antennae.

Hoverflies, also called "flower flies," mimic the appearance of bees and wasps. Unlike those stinging insects, however, flower flies are harmless. Adults feed on pollen and nectar.

Single pair of wings

The word *Diptera* means "two wings," which makes flies the only order of insects with a single pair of wings. Instead of a second pair of wings, flies have a pair of club-shaped organs called halteres. The halteres act as stabilizers that help flies balance in flight. The characteristic whine of midges and mosquitoes is produced by their rapidly beating wings. Hoverflies, as their name suggests, hover in front of flowers to collect nectar. They beat their wings furiously but remain stationary. Then, they dart away at speeds of up to 10 mph (16 kph). Flies have large compound eyes that occupy much of their head. The compound eyes provide excellent eyesight essential for high-speed flight.

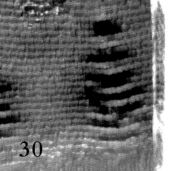

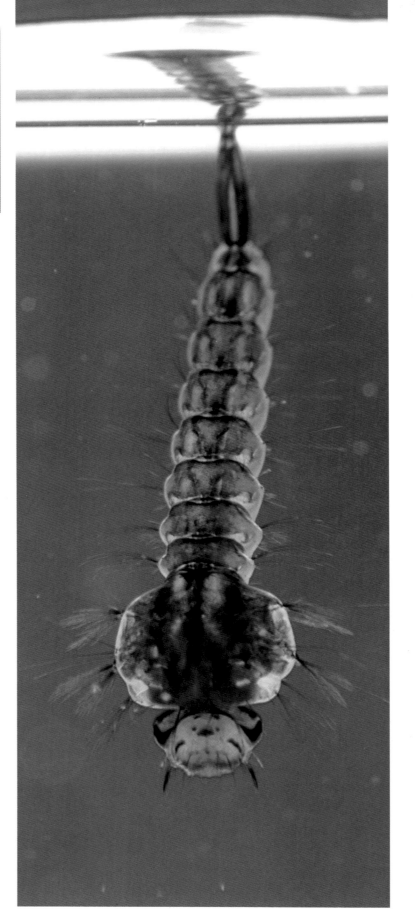

Life cycle

Flies undergo complete metamorphosis with four stages: egg, larva (maggot), pupa, and adult. The entire life cycle of a fly lasts between one and several weeks, depending on the species and temperature. Fly larvae, known as maggots, are legless and almost headless. The maggots turn into pupae, from which the adult flies emerge. Many flies lay their eggs in decaying animal matter and dung. Midges and mosquitoes lay their eggs in water. Parasitic flies lay their eggs in the living bodies of other animals. For example, the botfly lays its eggs in the nostrils of mammals, such as horses, sheep, and goats. The larvae hatch and move to the intestines, where they feed and grow. Flesh fly eggs hatch inside the females, which then deposit their larvae into the wounds of vertebrate animals, including humans. They also parasitize spiders, snails, and worms.

A mosquito larva, like this one, feeds on organic particles in the water. It gets oxygen from the surface through a breathing tube.

Food and habitats

One reason flies are so successful is that the various species have adapted to survive in diverse habitats. They make use of many different food sources. Flies feed on a range of foods, such as dead animal remains, dung, plant sap, and blood. Their mouthparts are adapted for piercing or sucking.

Scorpion flies (*Harpobittacus tillyardi*) are predatory insects. They hang from plants by their front legs, leaving their other legs to catch prey. This scorpion fly has caught a bee with its hind legs.

Bloodsuckers

Bloodsucking insects, such as mosquitoes, have piercing mouthparts that pass through skin to reach blood vessels. Only the females are bloodsuckers. Mosquitoes are considered dangerous insects because they can carry organisms that cause diseases, such as malaria, yellow fever, and dengue fever. For instance, the female *Anopheles* mosquito can transmit the

Mosquitoes suck blood through their piercing mouthparts.

The mouthparts of the female mosquito function as needles that pierce the skin and pump saliva into the wound. Their saliva contains a substance that prevents blood from clotting, which allows them to suck up blood through a central tube.

microscopic parasite that causes malaria. This parasite lives in people's blood. If a female mosquito feeds on the blood of an infected person, it may transfer the parasite to the next person it bites.

Liquid feeders

Blowflies and related species have a sucking mouthpart called a proboscis. When these insects find a food source, they empty the contents of their stomach on the food to digest it. Once the food has been turned into a liquid, they suck it up. Blowflies feed on many foods, including animal dung and dead animal bodies, picking up bacteria as they feed. They can easily contaminate food in a kitchen.

Predators

A few flies are predators, killing their prey as they suck its blood. Empids, or dance flies, have a long proboscis that they use to stab prey. They suck fluids from an animal's body through their proboscis.

Extra order: Fleas (Siphonaptera)

Fleas are tiny insects with no wings and a body that is flattened on the sides. Fleas don't have compound eyes. Their most distinctive feature is a pair of long legs adapted for jumping. Fleas jump from the ground onto passing animals, or from animal to animal, including humans. They attach to an animal's skin and feed on its blood. After feeding, the fleas drop off. Their larvae feed on dried blood, dead skin cells, and other organic debris in nests and dens.

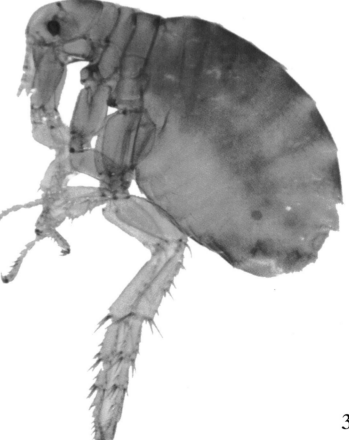

This flea, *Pulex irritans* (shown greatly enlarged), prefers human blood but also feeds on dogs, cats, and rats. Human flea infestations are uncommon among people who can bathe and wash their clothes regularly.

BUTTERFLIES AND MOTHS (LEPIDOPTERA)

A butterfly emerges from its pupal case. It must pump blood into its crumpled wings and allow them to dry before flying away.

Butterflies are some of the most beautiful insects in the world and often have large, colorful wings. They are closely related to moths, and together these two insect types form the order Lepidoptera. Butterflies and moths are found in all but the coldest parts of the world. Lepidoptera contains more than 165,000 different species, including the monarch, swallowtail, and red admiral butterflies, and the atlas and silk moths.

Lepidopteran features

Lepidoptera means "scale wing." Lepidopterans have two pairs of linked wings that are covered in tiny scales These scales—arranged in rows like roofing shingles—give the wing strength. The tubelike mouthparts of butterflies and moths, called a proboscis, is coiled up when not in use.

Complete metamorphosis

Lepidopterans undergo complete metamorphosis, with four stages: egg, caterpillar (larva), pupa, and adult. Adult butterflies and moths generally live only long enough to mate and for the females to lay eggs. The eggs hatch into caterpillars that have a cylindrical body with a head, thorax, and abdomen. They have three pairs of legs on their thorax and five pairs of prolegs, or false legs, on their abdomen. The caterpillar is the growing stage. When fully grown, it forms a pupa or chrysalis. This is the stage in which the caterpillar transforms into an adult butterfly or moth.

Wing colors

The colors of butterfly wings come from pigment in the scales and from the way light reflects off the surface of the scales. As light bounces off the irregular surface of the scales, it makes the blue morpho butterfly appear an iridescent blue. From above, the butterfly appears bright blue, but from the sides it looks violet.

The wingspan of the altas moth (*Attacus atlas*) measures up to 12 inches (30 cm) wide—about the size of a dinner plate.

Butterfly or moth?

Butterflies and moths are very similar in appearance and can be difficult to tell apart. In general, butterflies have clubbed antennae with rounded ends, long, thin bodies, and colorful wings. When still, they hold their wings upright so the undersides are exposed. Moths have fatter, hairier bodies. Their antennae are often feathery, but never clubbed. When still, moths spread their wings out, with the upper surface showing. In general, moths' wings come in drab colors, but there are some colorful exeptions. Butterflies are diurnal and fly during the day, while most moths are nocturnal, and fly at dusk or through the night.

KEY CHARACTERISTICS
LEPIDOPTERA

- **Two pairs of wings covered in scales.**
- **Mouthparts that form a proboscis.**
- **Complete metamorphosis.**

The silver-studded blue butterfly (*Plebejus argus*) is native to England. Its caterpillars feed on heather and other flowers.

Feeding

An adult butterfly or moth uses its long proboscis to reach deep inside flowers to feed on sweet plant juices, called nectar. Caterpillars resemble worms and feed on plant leaves. Their strong jaws are built for chewing. Most caterpillars eat the leaves of only one type of "host" plant, or group of plants. To make sure the caterpillars have enough food, the females lay eggs only on those types of plants. A number of species of butterflies, including the small tortoiseshell, red admiral, and peacock, may use the same host plant. Habitat preservation of the host plants is important because it has a direct impact on the distribution of a species. For example, the life cycle of the monarch butterfly (*Dannaus plexippus*) is closely linked to the availablity of milkweed plants.

The caterpillar of the spurge hawk moth (*Hyles Eupheriae*) has strong jaws to chew through tough leaves. It grips each leaf using the legs on its thorax and the prolegs on its abdomen.

Camouflage and warning colors

Butterflies, moths, and caterpillars are preyed upon by many animals, especially birds, so they have special ways to avoid predators. Some rely on coloring that blends in with their surroundings. Others rely on poisons and bright colors. The monarch butterfly and the garden tiger moth are poisonous. Their striking black and orange wings warn predators to stay away. To confuse predators, some caterpillars have false heads and antennae at the end of their abdomen. For instance, the puss moth caterpillar surprises predators by rearing up and waving its tail.

The caterpillar of the puss moth (*Cerura vinula*) has two tails at the end of its abdomen, which it whips into the air when disturbed by a predator.

Migration

Although most butterflies do not fly very far, monarch butterflies are an amazing exception. They journey thousands of miles (kilometers) from their summer breeding grounds to their winter roosting sites. During the summer months, these butterflies breed in the northern United States and in southern Canada. In the autumn, as the weather gets colder, they migrate south to the southern states and to Mexico, where they spend the winter roosting in trees. In the spring, the butterflies fly north again to find milkweed, the host plant of their caterpillars.

ANTS, BEES, AND WASPS (HYMENOPTERA)

Like termites, ants, bees, and wasps are social insects that live together in large groups, called colonies. Each colony feeds and cares for its larvae. Ants, bees, and wasps are considered the most advanced of all the insects. They live in a variety of habitats, including grasslands, woodlands, parks, and backyards.

Membrane wings

Ants, bees, and wasps belong to the order Hymenoptera, which consists of more than 225,000 species. Other members of the order include ants, honeybees, and ichneumon wasps. Hymenoptera means "membrane-like wings," which refers to these insects' nearly transparent, membranous wings. Tiny hooks join together the wings of these insects while in flight. Hymenopterans have both biting and sucking mouthparts. Bees, for example, have a pair of jaws for chewing and a long proboscis for sipping nectar from flowers. All members of this order undergo complete metamorphosis.

Wasps have powerful jaws and a short proboscis. They feed their larvae other insects and small invertebrates.

Hymenoptera is divided into two suborders, Symphyta and Apocrita. Symphyta is made up of the plant-eating sawflies. Apocrita contains ants, bees, and wasps, all of which have a narrow waist between the thorax and abdomen. Female ants, bees, and wasps have an ovipositor. This is an egg-laying structure that may also sting.

Workers, drones, and queens

Hymenopterans have a complex social structure made up of three classes, or castes. These are queens (fertile females), drones (males), and workers (infertile females). A colony of these social insects often includes thousands—and sometimes millions—of individuals. For example, a typical honeybee colony consists of a single queen, about three hundred male drone bees, and about fifty thousand worker bees. The queen is the only fertile female and is much larger than the other females. After mating, she starts laying up to two thousand eggs a day. Each worker bee has a particular job in the colony. Some clean and repair the cells of the hive, while others look after the larvae. Some are responsible for finding food. They leave the nest to find nectar and pollen. Others guard the nest.

Pollination

Ants, bees, and wasps play an important role in their habitat. For example, as bees or other similar insects feed on nectar, pollen sticks to their hairy bodies and transfers to the next flower, pollinating it. Without these helpful insects, many flowers could not produce seeds.

A beehive consists of a number of vertical honeycombs divided into thousands of hexagonal cells. The cells are used to store food and to provide a place to rear bee larvae.

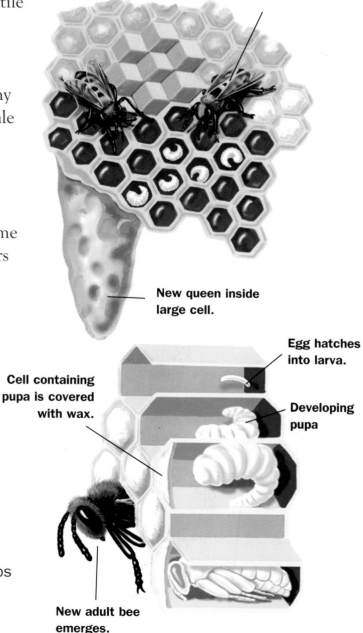

KEY CHARACTERISTICS
HYMENOPTERA

- **Complete metamorphosis.**
- **Members of Apocrita have a narrow waist between the thorax and abdomen.**
- **They are social insects.**

Cross Section of a Beehive

Worker bees feed honey and pollen to the larvae.

New queen inside large cell.

Cell containing pupa is covered with wax.

Egg hatches into larva.

Developing pupa

New adult bee emerges.

Armies of ants

Ants have poor eyesight. They rely on scent trails to find their way around. In a rain forest, huge colonies of army ants march across the forest floor looking for food. There may be as many as 700,000 individuals in a colony of army ants. Each day, raiding parties of approximately 150,000 ants leave the nest in a long column up to 328 feet (100 m) long and 26 feet (8 m) wide. Worker ants are virtually blind and follow the trail laid down by the scout workers. The ants prey on any animal they find in their path, small or large, insect or mammal. The prey is carried back along the trail to the nest. Army ants build huge nests in the forest, some of which extend as much as 20 feet (6 m) below the ground. They use these nests for a few weeks before moving on to a new nesting site.

Communication

As social insects, ants, bees, and wasps must communicate with one another. Ants communicate using a chemical, called a pheromone, produced from special glands. Worker ants use pheromones to mark their trails to the nest.

Meat ants (*Indomyrmex purpureus*) swarm over the carcass of a cricket many times their size. They tear the cricket apart and carry the pieces back to their nest.

40

Worker bees returning to the hive communicate the distance, direction, and quality of the food they discover by "dancing" or flying in a certain pattern. For example, a worker returning from a food source within 82 feet (25 m) of the hive performs a round dance with regular changes in direction. The more changes of direction, the better the quality of the food. If the food source is farther away, the worker bee does a waggle dance. In this, the bee moves in a figure eight. In the middle of the figure, the bee waggles its abdomen from side to side to indicate the distance of the food source. The number of times the bee repeats the dance indicates the quality of the food.

THE FIG WASP AND TREE

The fig wasp and the fig tree depend on each other for survival. The female wasp crawls inside the figs and lays eggs, pollinating the tiny flowers in the process. The figs provide a safe hiding place for the wasp's eggs and the tree benefits, too. Once the flowers are pollinated, they can produce seeds. The relationship between the fig wasp and the fig tree is an example of mutualism, in which both partners benefit from the situation.

Larval food

Bees feed their larvae pollen and honey. Wasps are predatory and feed their larvae meat. The female potter wasp lays its eggs within a clay, pot-shaped nest. It then catches a caterpillar or other prey and puts it in the pot beside the eggs. When the eggs hatch, the larvae feed on the caterpillar. The female ichneumon wasp goes to even greater lengths to provide food for larvae. This wasp lays its eggs in the bodies of other insects. When the eggs hatch, the larvae feed on the bodies of the insects, eventually killing them.

The potter wasp is a solitary wasp. The female builds a tiny nest out of mud to keep the egg safe.

UNDER THREAT

There are millions of different species of insects, but many are under the threat of extinction. The most threatened species are often the larger and more colorful insects, such as butterflies and beetles.

Habitat loss

One of the greatest threats to insects is the loss of habitat, especially tropical and temperate rain forests. Rain forests are home to more species of plants and animals than any other habitat. Scientists believe that millions of species—many of which are insects—are undiscovered. Some insect species have likely become extinct before biologists could discover them. Sadly, when one species disappears, others that depend on it may also disappear. For example, at least one hundred species of beetles, mites, and birds depend on the survival of the army ant (*Eciton burchelli*), found in Central and South America.

Many thousands of acres (hectares) of rain forest are cleared each year for lumber, farmland, and to make room for houses and roads.

Agricultural practices

Modern agriculture involves the use of chemicals, such as pesticides, to kill insect pests that damage crops. These chemicals often kill all insects, not just the pests. Useful insects, such as bees and ladybugs, are also killed.

Souvenirs

In many parts of the world, large butterflies and other interesting insects caught in the wild are sold as souvenirs. Such collecting from the wild threatens the survival of some of the more attractive insects. For example, the beautiful birdwing butterflies native to the rain forests of Southeast Asia are now endangered because of collection and rain forest clearance. Large beetles, such as the goliath beetle, are also endangered for the same reasons. Instead of removing these creatures from the wild, local people in some areas have set up butterfly breeding centers that sell such souvenirs to tourists.

Conserving insects

One of the ways to conserve a rare species is to breed it in captivity and then release it back into its natural habitat. Another way to help conserve insects is by releasing swarms of its natural enemies or by planting nearby vegetation that attracts the natural enemies. Scientists also closely monitor bioengineered food crops for their effects on valued insects, such as monarchs.

Butterflies collected in the wild are often sold as souvenirs to tourists.

BLUE BUTTERFLY

The large blue butterfly (*Maculinea arion*), became extinct in Britain in 1979. It survived elsewhere, but its disappearance from Britain baffled experts because plenty of suitable habitat remained. Scientists did not realize that the survival of *Maculinea arion* depended on a single species of red ants. In 2000, the first reintroductions of these butterflies took place at a number of sites where red ants were found. These reintroductions proved successful, and the butterfly is breeding again in Britain.

INSECT CLASSIFICATION

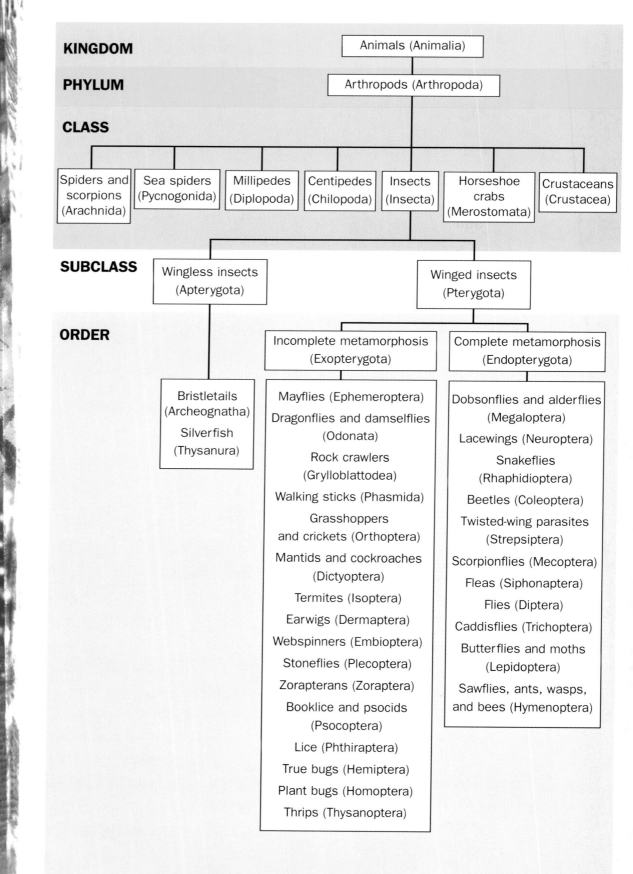

KINGDOM

Animals (Animalia)

PHYLUM

Arthropods (Arthropoda)

CLASS

| Spiders and scorpions (Arachnida) | Sea spiders (Pycnogonida) | Millipedes (Diplopoda) | Centipedes (Chilopoda) | Insects (Insecta) | Horseshoe crabs (Merostomata) | Crustaceans (Crustacea) |

SUBCLASS

Wingless insects (Apterygota)

Winged insects (Pterygota)

ORDER

Incomplete metamorphosis (Exopterygota)

Complete metamorphosis (Endopterygota)

Bristletails (Archeognatha)
Silverfish (Thysanura)

Mayflies (Ephemeroptera)
Dragonflies and damselflies (Odonata)
Rock crawlers (Grylloblattodea)
Walking sticks (Phasmida)
Grasshoppers and crickets (Orthoptera)
Mantids and cockroaches (Dictyoptera)
Termites (Isoptera)
Earwigs (Dermaptera)
Webspinners (Embioptera)
Stoneflies (Plecoptera)
Zorapterans (Zoraptera)
Booklice and psocids (Psocoptera)
Lice (Phthiraptera)
True bugs (Hemiptera)
Plant bugs (Homoptera)
Thrips (Thysanoptera)

Dobsonflies and alderflies (Megaloptera)
Lacewings (Neuroptera)
Snakeflies (Rhaphidioptera)
Beetles (Coleoptera)
Twisted-wing parasites (Strepsiptera)
Scorpionflies (Mecoptera)
Fleas (Siphonaptera)
Flies (Diptera)
Caddisflies (Trichoptera)
Butterflies and moths (Lepidoptera)
Sawflies, ants, wasps, and bees (Hymenoptera)

GLOSSARY

abdomen the third, or rear, part of an insect's body.

adapted changed in order to cope with the environment.

algae aquatic, plantlike organisms, from tiny, single-celled organisms to large seaweeds, such as kelp.

antennae the "feelers" on an insect's head, used to smell, touch, and taste.

aquatic growing or living in water.

arthropod an invertebrate animal with an exoskeleton and jointed limbs, such as a crab, spider, insect, or centipede.

brood chamber a protected place where eggs and larvae develop.

camouflage colors and patterns that allow an insect or other animal to blend in with its background.

carnivorous meat-eating.

carrion dead or decaying flesh.

caterpillar the larva of a butterfly or moth.

cerci structures that extend from the end of the abdomen of some insects, such as earwigs and bristletails.

colony a large group of insects that live together, such as ants and termites.

compost a mixture of decaying organic matter, such as leaves and food waste.

compound eye an insect eye made up of a large number of tiny units.

contaminate to make impure.

diurnal active during the day.

dung the droppings (feces) of animals.

evolve to slowly change over a long period of time and throughout several generations.

evolution the process of slow, gradual change over time.

exoskeleton the rigid skeleton on the outside of an insect's body.

extinct no longer in existence.

fertile able to reproduce.

forceps a pair of pincers or tongs, used for grasping.

fungus (plural: fungi) an organism that is neither plant nor animal and is placed in its own kingdom. Yeasts, molds, and mushrooms are all fungi.

gills organs used to absorb oxygen from water, present in aquatic insect larvae.

habitat the natural environment of a plant or animal.

halteres the modified hind wings of flies that are used as balancing organs.

herbivore an animal that eats plants.

hexagonal six-sided.

invertebrate an animal without a backbone, such as an insect or a snail.

larva one of the immature stages in the life cycle of an insect that undergoes complete metamorphosis.

lichen an organism that lives on a hard surface and looks like a plant, but is an alga and a fungus living together.

maggot another name for a larva, particularly a fly larva.

malaria a disease transmitted by mosquitoes that causes fever and chills.

mammal a hair-covered vertebrate that feeds its young milk.

mask the extendable lower lip of dragonfly and damselfly nymphs used for seizing prey. When not in use, the mask folds back and covers the insect's mouthparts.

GLOSSARY (CONTINUED)

metamorphosis a series of changes in body shape during the life cycle from larva to adult. Complete metamorphosis involves four stages, while incomplete metamorphosis has three stages.

migrate to make a regular journey from one place to another.

molt when used in connection with insects, to shed the exoskeleton.

nocturnal active at night.

nymph the larva of an insect that undergoes incomplete metamorphosis.

omnivore an animal that eats both plants and animals.

order a category of organisms in the system of classification, ranking above a family and below a class.

ovipositor egg-laying organ.

parasite an organism that lives on or in another organism and causes that organism harm.

pheromone a body chemical used to attract a mate or for communication.

phylum the main division of a kingdom in the system of classification, ranking above a class.

pitch the highness or lowness of a sound, determined by the number of vibrations producing it.

predator an animal that catches and kills other animals.

prey an animal that is caught and killed by a predator.

primitive at an early stage of evolution or development; for example, bristletails are considered more primitive than butterflies.

proboscis the long, thin mouthpart structure used by flies, butterflies, and moths to suck up nectar.

prolegs fleshy structures that resemble legs; found on the abdominal segments of insects.

pronotum the upper surface of the first thoracic segment of insects that may extend forward over the head or backward to cover the thorax.

pupa the third stage in the life cycle of an insect undergoing complete metamorphosis.

rain forest diverse, dense forestland that receives high amounts of precipitation; found in tropical and temperate regions.

rostrum mouthparts that protrude beyond the front of an animal and often resemble a beak.

scavenge to feed on dead or decaying matter.

sp. an abbreviation for "species," used as part of the Latin name for animals when the exact species is unknown.

species a group of organisms with similar characteristics that can only breed successfully with one another.

stridulation the process by which certain insects produce sounds.

stylets the piercing mouthparts of insects, such as aphids.

thorax the middle part of the body of an arthropod.

FURTHER INFORMATION

BOOKS

Aloian, Molly. *The Life Cycle of a Beetle. Life Cycle* (series). Crabtree (2004).

Butterflies of the World. Fandex Family Field Guides. Workman Publishing (2002).

Jackson, Donna M. *The Bug Scientists. Scientists in the Field* (series). Houghton Mifflin (2004).

Kirkland, Jane. *Take a Walk with Butterflies and Dragonflies. Take a Walk* (series). Soundprints (2004).

Kneidel, Sally. *More Pet Bugs: A Kid's Guide to Catching and Keeping Insects and Other Small Creatures.* Wiley (1999).

Markel, Sandra. *Outside and Inside Killer Bees.* Walker & Company (2004).

Mound, Laurence. *Insect. Eyewitness Books* (series). Dorling Kindersley (2004).

Murawski, Darlyne A. *Bug Faces.* National Geographic (2000).

Scholl, Elizabeth J. *Praying Mantis. Bugs* (series). Kidhaven Press (2004).

Wright, Anne, ed. *Insects: The Plant and Animal Kingdoms.* Discovery Channel School Science (series). *Gareth Stevens (2002).*

WEB SITES

http://animaldiversity.ummz.umich.edu/site/accounts/information/Insecta.html
Follow the various links to explore the sights and sounds of the insect world.

www.butterflyworld.com/campaign.html
Click on your state to see how you can help the butterflies in your area.

www.dragonflies.org/faq.htm
Find the answers to frequently asked questions about dragonflies.

www.earthlife.net/insects/six.html
Visit the Wonderful World of Insects to learn more about these fascinating creatures.

www.ecokidsonline.com/pub/fun_n_games/games/bugHunt/index.cfm#
Advance through several levels as you find the bugs in these gardens.

www.forensicentomology.com/
Discover how insects can help police track down criminals.

www.mnh.si.edu/museum/VirtualTour/Tour/Second/InsectZoo/insect4.html
Take a virtual tour of the insect exhibit at the National Museum of Natural History.

www.orkin.com/learningcenter/kidsandteachers_games.asp
Test your insect-identification skills when you play "Name That Insect."

INDEX

Page numbers in **bold** refer to a photograph or illustration.

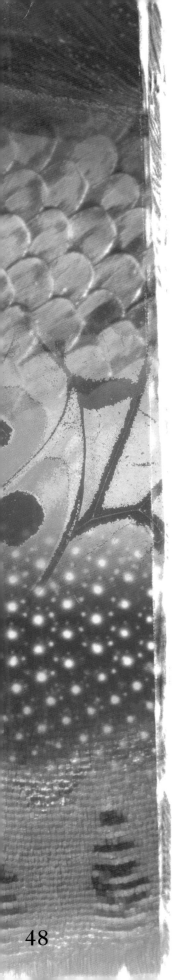